Acknowledgment: photographs on page 4 (top) and
page 5 (top) used by courtesy of Eastern Counties Newspapers

All Ladybird books are available at most bookshops,
supermarkets and newsagents, or can be ordered direct from:

Ladybird Postal Sales
PO Box 133 Paignton TQ3 2YP England
Telephone: (+44) 01803 554761
Fax: (+44) 01803 663394

A catalogue record for this book is available
from the British Library

Published by Ladybird Books Ltd
A subsidiary of the Penguin Group
A Pearson Company
© LADYBIRD BOOKS LTD MCMXCVII

Diana

Princess of Wales

By AUDREY DALY
with photographs by
TIM GRAHAM

As a child

She was beautiful, she was glamorous – and she was loved the world over for her warm heart and her generosity. The girl who became in her short life the People's Princess was born Lady Diana Spencer, on 1st July 1961. She was the third daughter of Earl Spencer

A cuddle for her guinea pig 'Peanuts'

The Spencer family home, Althorp

and his first wife. Although the family home was Althorp in Northamptonshire, Diana spent a lot of time on the Queen's estate at Sandringham. She played with Prince Andrew and Prince Edward – and she called their mother 'Aunt Lilibet'.

At 17, bridesmaid at her sister's wedding

The teen years

Diana was never academic. She was a quiet, shy girl who loved music and ballet – and young children. So when she left Westheath School in 1977 (the year she met Prince Charles), she took a job as a nursery teacher in Pimlico. She wasn't there long before rumours began to spread about a

Diana in her very first job at the Young England Kindergarten in Pimlico

Diana's father, Earl Spencer

possible romance with the heir to the throne.
But the romance was slow to start. Then she
went for a holiday to the Queen's Scottish
home, Balmoral. The Royal watchers woke up.
At one bound, Diana took centre stage in the
spotlight of press attention.

Diana's school, Westheath

Courting

Privacy was a thing of the past. Wherever Diana went – shopping, going to work or out for the evening – there was always someone with a camera not far away.

The rumours strengthened, and Diana had to cancel a skiing holiday because of the publicity.

Some sneaked photographs

Diana's London flat, which she shared with friends. Her red Metro was always parked opposite.

Then at last, in February 1981, the engagement between Charles and Diana was announced. All seemed set for a happy ending. They planned to marry on 29th July.

The ring she wore with pride...

And still more photographers...

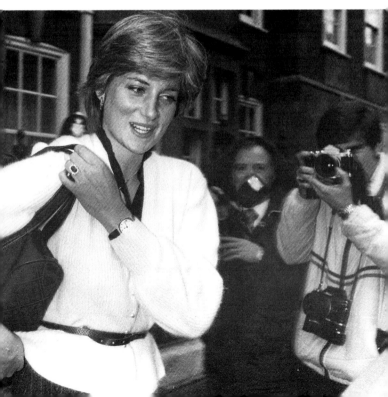

The Royal Wedding

The world looked forward to Diana's wedding, and loved every minute. Seven hundred million people around the globe watched the ceremony on television. The service was relayed to the huge crowds outside St Paul's Cathedral, who could be heard joining in the responses.

Diana's first moments as HRH The Princess of Wales

Children of her own

Diana was a happy woman when her children came along. She proved to be a watchful, caring mother who gave them a great deal of time. When her first son William was only a baby, she and Charles even took him on an Australian trip.

The fun years with her children, Prince William and Prince Henry (Wills and Harry to their mother!)

Leading fashion

Wherever Diana went, women were eager to see what she was wearing. Her hairstyles, shoes, jewelry and indeed her entire wardrobe were admired and copied.

In Wellington, New Zealand

At Ascot races

In Egypt

In London at the Barbican for the Hong Kong Gala Evening

In Brussels

In Nigeria

Friends

Diana's friends were legion, from all walks of life. But the famous were charmed by her warmth as well, loving her sincerity. Wherever she went, people sought her company.

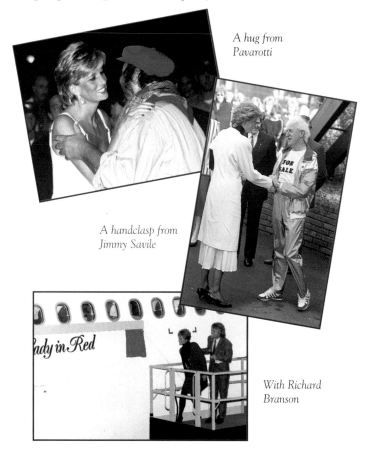

A hug from
Pavarotti

A handclasp from
Jimmy Savile

With Richard
Branson

Dancing with John Travolta

Sale of the century...

With the end of a disappointing marriage, Diana's lifestyle began to change. She attended few gala occasions unless they were in connection with a charity she supported.

Eventually, seventy nine of her truly glamorous gowns were sold at auction. People flocked to buy, and the huge sums raised went to charity.

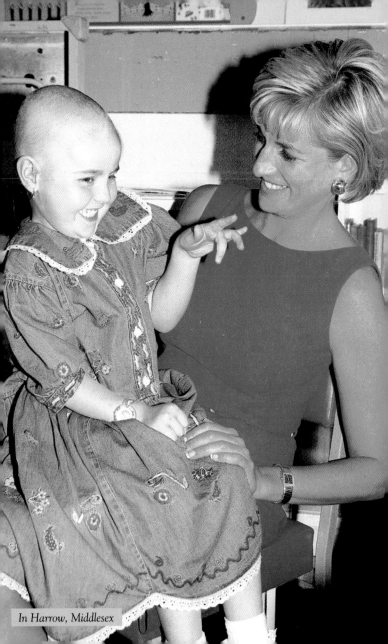
In Harrow, Middlesex

A helping hand around the world

Slowly, Diana came to terms with a different kind of life. She went out to people who needed her. She knew she could help, and that sometimes just a gentle touch could improve things. People who needed comfort often found her close by.

In Portland, Australia

In Newfoundland

In Wales

In Hong Kong

At the Leprosy Hospital
in Jakarta

Opening the Red Cross
Centre in Derbyshire

In Hungary

In Chicago

THE HOSPITAL

The children's hospital
at Great Ormond Street
was one of Diana's
favourite charities

At Mother
Theresa's
Hospice in
Calcutta

Helping the
homeless

Cuddling a child with
HIV in Brazil

Diana felt very strongly about the use of landmines and the harm they caused. She spearheaded a worldwide campaign to ban their use

In Angola, with 13 year old Sandra Thijika, who lost one of her legs in a landmine explosion

Working with the Red Cross in Angola

The People's Princess, 1961-1997

Diana, Princess of Wales was exquisitely lovely
and a joy to look at. She was also kind,
courageous and deeply honest. The whole world
misses her. She lives on in our hearts.

Her 36th birthday